Constellations

Maxi Fanelli

Presentation by *BookLeaf Publishing*

Web: www.bookleafpub.com

E-mail: info@bookleafpub.com

ISBN:9789358314984

First edition 2024

DEDICATION

To Jorge Luis Borges and Gustavo Cerati, building bridges between British and Latin culture.

To my mother, for giving me the surname.

To the constellation of Columba, In Total Aspiration.

And to you. For motivating me, giving me courage and showing me humanity.

Just Two

A murmur,
a mirror,
trembling palpitations,
in desire.
Paintings,
illusions on a crystal,
dancing a minimal ritual.

A roar,
coined from a reflection,
The sweet summit,
our time standing still.

Our skin.
Dim dawns in lust.
On a blanket, our thirst.

Someone is staring at us
Someone is staring at us
Someone is staring at us
What does he see?
Vivid lust reflections

Roar.
We open our eyes.

We see the whispers
of this alchemy
Caressing,
that veil that conceal us,
enshrouds animal vibes.

We do not care
We do not care
We do not care
No thirst.
Reflections, more than lust
In two, just two.

Beyond time,
we stopped time
we saw ourselves traveling,
over thousands of reflections.

In two, just two.
To be in two.-

When the body speaks

You speak, with your body
You pray, with your skin
You crave, wrapped in fright.
You atomise love on a nebula,
When a quasar beams solitude.
You speak, with your body,
You whisper, with your skin,
You hurt, in escapism.
Daydreams, with no deserving.
Afterlife premonitions,
of my other true self.

Breeze, the summit of your silence.
Murmurs, with no rubs from your skin.
Sparks, of your blinding whispers.
Blind, I am lost in my own faith.

You spoke, with your skin.
You moaned, with your demons.
I ripped, your wicked shield
A gateway to another universe,
where you got yourself locked away.

To forget your body
is to forget your verb,

Your real inner self,
clumsily reverberates.
A silent drug in my veins,
floating between heaven and hell.

Getting lost in downfall,
speaking the language of our bodies.
One last time,
reciting a transcendental poem.
All our senses overloaded,
All our mysteries drained,
Two oceans in sour tears.
It is just your verb and mine as well.
Our infinity, our end.-

Delayed minor chords

Your smiles, gilded with craze.
My guitar, a spectre in your room.
Minor chords, craving your pillow.
Sparkles of a temporal line
bring a future in stillness.

Stranded dreams in a melodic river,
wildly flowing in scales with sixths.
Lulls of minor ninths
when your curls I caress.
A dominant in climax then,
A timeless riddled music sheet.

Four hands piano,
offbeat enchanted melodies,
Jazz in runaway alterations,
quit, escape, ignore.
One last seventh minor bold chord.

A simple major arpeggio brings us back.
A Bloody Sunday with *No Surprises*
Both in lust, in music, sheer peace.
Distance, one million light years away
an eerie silent note in this pentagram.

A voice,
a flower,
a teacher
our cause,
in doubt.

Only in sorrow I can sing
an intense deafening shout.
I write over your ghostly veil,
a symphony with delayed minor chords.

Hypnotised under a temporal trance,
I discover crossing parallel lines,
on this singular infinity.
When your body speaks and your soul conceals.-

Ever after

Ever after,
when everything is gone,
droplets of your perfume,
your floating pictures,
your true self.

We confessed everything we were,
we hushed what we may be
we whispered an utopic gale.

Ever after,
it is hard to say it,
say it without saying it,
what kindly forced us to do it.

A maiden flight,
a future to be brushed,
my piano under wicked sorcery,
the fever of those days,
blurred memories of laughter.
I shall give it all
fall asleep on you,
wake up on us.
Expecting it will finally be,
be different from yesterday.

Ever after,
it might be real,
when we were lost,
we broke resignation,
We craved stimulation,
floating with no demands,
accepting with no remorse.

Ever after,
we will become
what we will become.-

Wishful thinking

No tale on a loop,
we softly melted,
we kindly possessed ourselves,
our sorcery on a loop.

Both hypnotised
with darts on poisonous fears,
with prayers on kisses,
just like heaven.

Over my cyclothymia I write
words in continuous movement,
Dizzed into the unknown.

Tribulation,
the labyrinth of our fears.
What do you see?
Using your doubt as a rose.

Your magnetic appeal,
sharp spine
seethes the tip of my fingers.

Natural drug
pouring through my veins.

Rapted sap.
My words,
your personal diary,
an enigmatic code.

Lying to myself,
I feel all that it is thirst
Stepping up,
I feel everything that still has not been.
Shouting up,
my naked soul shows everything I feel.
Climbing higher and higher,
when you still feel that I am in you.

Our mantra

This charming sea
choked you inside me.
You can still barely breathe.
Staggering, trembling.

Depths.
Bonding, droplets of air,
just us inside our bubble,
subtle moments of life.

I barely wish
this sort of wishful thinking.-

In the pond

I see your quietness from the shore
I see your wet lips mirrored
In such a naive manner,
algae covering your true self.
So many people craving your skin.

From the shore of the pond
I see people craving only your skin.

I spring, like a seabird I am diving now.
Stars that cuddle me, as your blonde curls do.
They stare at me, they touch me, they haunt me
In this daydream velvet blue pond.

So many people before me,
So many people in this pond.

Leather, leaves, nails…
in the end,

it will only be about your pale cheeks.
Sinking myself,
it is only your air that I can breathe.
Only answers I find in the depths.
In the depths,
under the surface,
of this bittersweet daydream.

I keep on swimming,
I sense your calmness.
I keep on swimming,
I feel your calmness,
while I stop breathing.-

My infrared sight

My infrared sight.
I fear,
I loose,
I suffer,
I idealise,
While seeing deeper than you ever could
With my infrared sight.

My infrared sight
unveils the heat your body speaks.
In desperation you try to cover,
Dispeling radiation,
tears my inner skin apart.

My infrared sight
translates the hieroglyphics,
drawn in your skin.
It is always today,
not a surprise anymore.
I touch them in surreal animations.
In my dreams.

My infrared sight
sees through the walls of your volcano
Honey lava

Impossible to taste
sinful temptation.

My infrared sight,
sees your gravity centre.
Singular metamorphosis, Gregor.
On this alchemy pictured in poetry
lies visions of my infrared sight,
breaking into your skin,
cracking your marrow,
forcing you to escape.

My infrared sight
Keeps seeing even light years away.
Your cruelty,
your cowardice,
your contradictions.
I can even see you
blinded by the heat you cast.
Burning ashes for years.

My infrared sight
Sees your life in litmus
Sunlight rays sparkling your eyes
A messy web of fibres at their highest tension,
everything I trembled in you,
that delusional litmus aura.

My infrared sight,

I can see through skin,
I can see through your skin.
You cannot cover it
Not even the distance,
Not even your silence.
Your inner self.
Sensorial radioactivity.

My infrared sight
sees much more that you can see
much more that you can stand
Fear and surrender.-

Boreal fable

Boreal fable
Such coldness, decoupled.

She can only escape
when all that she wants
is to wake up for you.

Boreal fable
There are no words,
only delayed minor chords.

Sweet whispers hold
our pole in mellow lights.

I do not know what the end will look like
I want to see the truth in our eyes
We are trapped in an avalanche on a loop
We are free in our souls in hunger.

Boreal fable,
walking over the edge of our void.
She wants to believe in her will,
I want to believe in my dream

I do not want to think in the end.

I just want to rest inside you.
First or last tipping point.
Only tonight the Northern Lights will guide

Destroying time inside crystal bubbles
Drawing a magnetic sky above us

No words to paint
Frosted sounds emerge
Closing our eyes, create
Fantasise

We are ghosts
Fantasising
Lost
A morning star
A comet
A northern light
A path
A cause
We found ourselves
Flowing
Growing.-

Thirst

A wild storm,
in kindness our ocean burns.
A coded signal,
you could swiftly escape from this saltless sea.
Your mysterious fragility,
flourishes in dreams of outer worlds.
Brakes in waves, contortates and hypnotises.
Haunted, you draw an occultism,
it will make you break your security,
it will make you shout in your ritual,
it will make you travel through your loneliness.

Who will be your escapism muse?

You will slow down,
surfing that unreal nirvana.

You will cocktail,
acids and algae in excess.
Just to escape today
in a giant leap to redemption.

These are your submission days,
you shall do everything to fly away,
from the fiction and delusion,
on your planet with no truths.

Where you will lose your life,
drinking the deceptive potion.
Where you will lie to yourself,
believing your sky is The sky.
But it will never…

Be flooded by our sea
Be dried by our thirst.-

The garden with converging walkaways

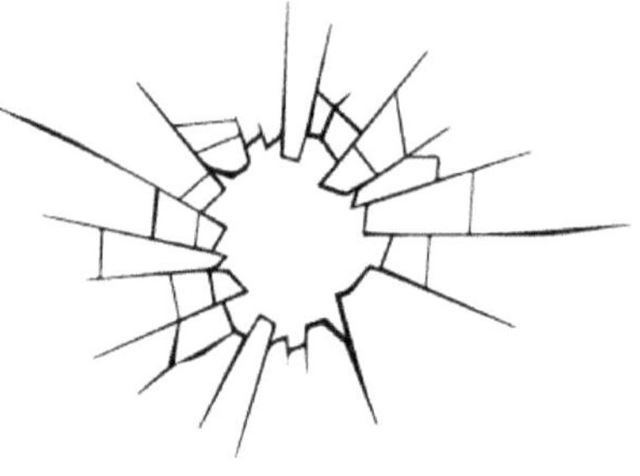

The deity on an urge,
The evil at his mercy,
They both conspired with irony,
over virtue and sin.

A sofa suddenly morphed,
endless walkaways,
merging in a bubble,
shielded from time.

It is so real.

We saw our pasts,
in all their universes,
nothing could have been,
in all their infinites.

We saw our futures,

everything can and cannot exist,
quantum conundrum,
searching for our temporal line,
such a Villain is hunting us.
Our demons.
The Demon.

Jumping to another universe
Where everything could be.
Numbed and ravished,
hyper stimulation,
contradictory epiphanies,
our energy in suspension.

Realistic utopies,
a quantic truth,
fears and more fears,
jumping between universes,
freezing our moments as one.

Bring back them on a loop,
looking for our timeline,
as Hans in the garden did.

Traveling beyond
imagination,
parallel reality,
becomes so real.-

Scars

Scars, carved on torn skin
with the blade of that game.
An inconsistency arises.
In my dream for you,
In my endless ego.

Scars, a pain from the past.
Drawn in weak flesh
Impracticable illusion
Sank everything in oblivion
Everything is floating again.

The spirits living in the night
cannot hold anymore
the darkness that sees
when finally breaks the day.
Existentialism lights are mere scars,
wounds that this world has seen arising in
gloom.

Scars from thwarted love
Hackneyed alibi
Escapism from that freedom
That keeps us apart

Masking all truth.

Scars for every lie
Scattered all over this Earth
If I could just heal you
With the strength of my voice.
With my words on enlightenment,
With my words in passion.-

Sacro-species

A ritual, broken freedom.
The social grandiose game,
paganic deceitful masks,
surrounding sensuality,
And so I am…

Tossing and turning
Tossing and turning

Believing in love,
such a delusion,
a sad simulation.
Pain, loneliness and selfishness
are the only twisting human forces.

Tossing and turning
Tossing and turning

I refuse to stop dreaming,
crossing the line will only disturb you,
In that end,
a mere mellow ritual.

Estranged by this tribe,
I fear, I am part of their clan

Morphing myself into a sacro-species
At the centre of their ritual

Tossing and turning
Tossing and turning.-

Sarcastic paradoxes

A vision on demand
A perfect way to understand
That your hands are empty
When it is all nothing but a game.

A miracle in demand
A perfect way to grow
a sense of weak understanding
What keeps you away
From changing your reality.

A wonder in demand
A perfect way of carving daylight
when you breathe darkness outside

Turning your own misery into a perfect drug.

A virtue on demand
A perfect way to clear the path
From the shadows of your soul
With a higher bright,
blinding your diminished sight.

Sarcastic paradox
when happiness is on the scene
where all trues lie deep down the sea
What it is false is despised.-

Escape

Wake up,
stare at the dream that you are leaving behind.
Walk on,
hypnotic whispers floating here and now.
Sail away,
without seeing the wind that bends you.
Unfitted here,
When all sense has been lost.

What do you see?
In your dreams,
In your longins.
What do you believe?
from what you have been given and told.

The truth,
that will finally break you free.
May it be,
what will forever lock away your emotions.
You blink,
on a belief that it all will settle down.
Concealing,
an internal blaze consumes you.

What do you see?
Linked, on a trance

What will you believe?
Walking. Uncovering

Existential game.
Hesitation.
Doubts
There is something beyond
Over and above.-

Learning to pretend

If my fears were only about turmoil
then desire could only mean demise.
You run away from me,
you run away from you.
You fear for me,
you cry for yourself.
I tried to wishful think even further
until I finally sunk,
in you,
on me.
Trying to make sense of such a marbled mirage.
Flying on that beloved demise

Recurrent emotions I foresee.
Constellation of noises about to explode.
I lie to myself while learning to pretend.

Fooling myself with this deceit,

disguising you, I dread on me.
You hold me far away, so close.
Escapism on an endless journey.
Let time carve a forbidden silhouette,
on me,
in you.
Flying, there is no ground underneath.
Recurrent emotions I foresee.
Constellation of noises about to explode
I lie to myself while learning to pretend
Sealed emotions, a pleasant deception.

I lie alongside your fears.
With deep mercy,
constellations of white noise,
this sky in flames will sob us.
With no pain,
this sky in flames will burn us.-

Andromeda

I opened my eyes after an eternal passage.
I did not want to caress the daylight
I feel you as real as an embodied mystery.
A marble brush drawing,
our bodies in entanglement.
It was another daydream in Andromeda
In Andromeda, nebulas and giant stars.

I might make you happy in a distant galaxy
I might make you happy on that planet
It is in Andromeda.
I might make you happy only in that daydream
when all I want is to close my eyes,
and let my mind wander away.

The dream echoed on a chain reaction,
On that planet that held our moaning cries.

You used to whisper, a melody dying in the air.
Light years away,
 I cannot lose my life on the journey
While I see you frozen
Overwhelmed by the ordinary

I would not want to wake up,
A calm daydream light years away

Everything comes to an end
right after the journey into deep space.
Everything comes to an end
right after flying into the Andromeda Nebulas.
Today your elitism is submission,
and I cannot break your shell
to let your soul wander away.-

Limit (I must find)

On this sea of chords,
with guitars I am floating now
Trying to link my aura to what it was
Wrapped around that sorcery game,
I am scribbling our yesterdays

It seems I am
with no compass wandering on high seas
Coming back on a winding path,
the tide pushes me further away

Penelope she was and will be,
In a garden, a dream.
I strive up to that limit,
but she will always remain with me.

Dulcinea come to me,
foresee what I shall be.
Desdemona she is here,
but I will escape from her cage.
Penelope she was,
it was late when I found myself on her.
I cannot breathe no more,
pale blue high sea.

Penelope she was and will be

In a garden, a daydream.
I strive up to that limit
I cannot swim back to you
A limit I must find.-

Golden nuggets

Your master riddle shatters my ego.
Your secret deafens me with its white noise.
A labyrinth with just one exit in its centre.
Your tumultuous riddled inner self.
Filtering noise and mud with a sieve
until I finally grab your golden nuggets,
until I finally grab your bitter stones.

Your smooth skin,
goosebumps in synchronism
Your hot body when we wake up
Holding your small hands
Travelling through your cheeks
the air you exhale on my neck
A Bubbled Peace,

carries us away to another universe.

Laugh about simplicity,
Relativise complexity.
See the world with enlightened glasses.
Your lips on my lips,
stop the bleeding.
You wear my love on a black velvet dress
Kiss you one more time,
as if it was the last time
One more time
One more night
The final night will come.
But not tonight.

Our verbs censored by your shame
Your curls in my pillows
Unplanned disposals
Reminiscences of a tricky spell
That we still cannot name it.
An endless hour of our bodies intertwined.

After love, we sing in the dark
We do not realise our bodies are merged.
Merged in the heat of a mismatched tune.
Eerie distance is now breaking us apart.
A paradise turned into jungle in downfall
We break ourselves apart,
in the corners of this mysterious paths,

indolence paths.

Natural forces both attract and repel us
Twisting magnetic poles
Light blue pearls in the floor
attached to the fragments of a broken jar.

A sky with electrified clouds
The sky is waiting for us,
fly-by.
Birds join us with a charming melody
That was our way,
elevate ourselves in wonder melodies
My songs, your petite hands in my hands
Naked, I embraced you from your back
Foreseeing a faint future,
on a small window, the river.
Waiting for a new night
Its darkness will calm us both down
Its darkness will fulfil us
forever and ever.

Blue hearts in cold,
pale mirror of our chimaera,
a cannon in offbeated repetition,
a deliberated offbeat imbalance.

Flickering, blinking
again your quasar flies away

at the beat of the universe in expansion
Cruelly hypnotising me
When I find your eyes in the sky,
Surrounded and hidden by a trillion stars.
While we are a million light years away.

Reminiscences of the *Winged Man*
He inspires us to carve,
To carve such a spell
Our spell
Caressed us, carried us
In a glider to a supernova.
Our glider.

Who shall know what we will become?
Your golden nuggets are like bread crumbs
Leave me in hunger
Leave me in thirst.
All the bliss that it is to come
That shall never come
That will perhaps arise.-

Grounding

I see,
winds that face me
I know,
I kick the horizon
of my true self
I understand that time is all
And it is relative.
But I do not know
How can I live without you
even if I know
That we might be fine
this time
Or in no other time
Or in any other life
Or in any other Universe.
Give ourselves time, a sandwatch.
Frozen sand in relativity.

I cannot stand anymore
Our demons in rage
They will not loosen up their grip
Until we surrender to their will
And melt our bodies in eternal lust

Maybe,

this is all my own madness
on this damned Island

Days on submission
Contemplation fires
No grounded energy
Flames that burn us
Reflections that guide us,
to our dimension,
Rescuing, soothing us.

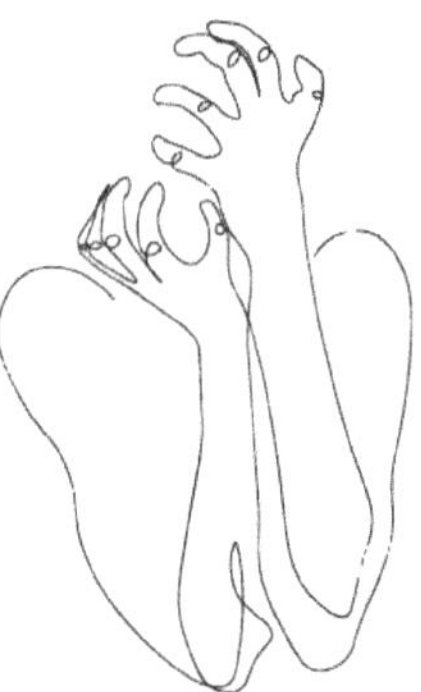

Peace.
A kind of paradise
Cast on a blurry substance
In myself,
in all the distance,
on that mirror.
Un-unplug ourselves.
Now.-

Stalemate

Stalemate.
My recursive movements,
your repeated evasions.
No checkmate shall be claimed,
fearing we will finally be together.
No checkmate shall be claimed,
fearing everything will finally end.

Stalemate.
No motion, over centuries.
Trapped, alienated, numbed.
No cure.
No relief.
At the mercy of your cruelty,
you will kick the board.
One more time

Stalemate.
No winning, no losing.
Facing us, only you and me.
Facing us, beholding us.
Fearing one more movement,
fearing one more hurt,
fearing to resume,
a new game,
a new life.

Stalemate
White moves,
Black escapes,
Never-ending story.-

The End

In the end
Dominant seventh, strident.
Absent tonic, no rest.

In the end
Wake up from a dream, never to sleep again.
Forever opened eyes, no blinks.
Shutdown consciousness, no memories.

In the end.
One last note, remorses.
Then time, forever stopped.
My memories,
they will only remain in others
Our memories,
they will only remain in you.
Until your end finally breaks them away.

Before the end.
Eternal life, arrogance.
Paradise, unimagined.
The harm that I caused you
Paradise, undeserved.
Detaches me from today,
from yesterday,

from tomorrow,
from you.

After the end.
My successes and failures, they shall remain
on only a few more droplets of time.
No more forgiveness, no more praise.
I will never see again the smiles I draw in you,
I will never see again the teardrops I pulled out
from you.

In the end.
Jumping into the void, a new world.
That nobody knew, nor knows,
nor will ever know about.
Aftermath, afterlife.
I will find you there, maybe.
Everything will go away, perhaps.

After the end.
What we have been, will slowly fade away.
No time, no going back.
Everlasting hell,
everlasting penance,
Such is the pain we brought to ourselves.

In the end.
Bravery,
desperation,

remorse,
incompleteness.
Nothing in everything.

Before the end.
My life, seized.
Daydreams,
pristine.
Detached from today,
Detached from yourself.

After the end.
All that I longed for,
All that I dreamt,
All that I laughed about,
All that I suffered,
All that I loved you
Will disappear.
After your end,
nothing will remain.

In the end.
Goodbye, I say to you.
Maybe, I yearn for it.
At last, I shut myself down.-

Mantra (encore)

I foresee with my mantra,
I stop time with my mantra
Blindly moving on,
Leaving it all behind.
Movements under a frozen spell

Making my peace with time
I am in debt with my dreams.
Freedom in strength,
Alternative horizons,
An endless peace.

What is subtle, is beautiful.
Beauty is subtle, in peace.
Painting distant horizons
In fractals with no clouds,
Using my endless pallet

A special kind of mandala.
I am losing myself,
I am carrying myself,
With no sense of time,
With no sense of space.

What is subtle, is beautiful
Beauty is subtle, in peace

Ticking salty seconds
completely dried my mouth,
built a hundred deserts
that finally quenched my thirst.
A special kind of lust,
With no sense of time,
With no sense of space.

What is subtle, is beautiful
Beauty is subtle, in peace

Time resumes

I open the mystical sense,
an incomprehensible freedom.
I cannot even paint it,
I can fully imagine it,
keeping my eyes shut
With no sense of time.
With no sense of space

Repeating my mantra

What is subtle, is beautiful
Beauty is subtle, in peace

If I were to breath
in just the first second
the air of all human times
the air of all human dreams
If I were to find
in such that second
that all my promises
were the mantra of this present
and the mirror of my era

So then I will dare to find,
So then I will dare to see,
So then I will dare to paint,
my future.

My Tomorrow…

9 789358 314984